BA BRAIN ACADEMY

SUPERMATHS

GW00503750

Louise Moore
and Richard Cooper

Mission File 1

Years 2-3

Produced in association with

National Association
for Able Children
in Education

RISING STARS

Rising Stars are grateful to the following people for their support in developing this series: Sue Mordecai, Julie Fitzpatrick, Johanna Raffan, Belle Wallace and Clive Tunnicliffe.

NACE, PO Box 242, Arnolds Way, Oxford OX2 9FR
www.nace.co.uk

Rising Stars UK Ltd, 22 Grafton Street, London W1S 4EX
www.risingstars-uk.com

Every effort has been made to trace copyright holders and obtain their permission for the use of copyright materials. The authors and publisher will gladly receive information enabling them to rectify any error or omission in subsequent editions.

All facts are correct at time of going to press.

Published 2007
Text, design and layout © Rising Stars UK Ltd.

Editorial Consultant: Jean Carnall
Cover design: Burville-Riley
Design: Pentacor**big**
Illustrations: Cover – Burville-Riley / Characters – Bill Greenhead

British Library Cataloguing in Publication Data.
A CIP record for this book is available from the British Library.

ISBN: 978-1-84680-230-0

Printed by Craft Print International Ltd, Singapore

CONTENTS

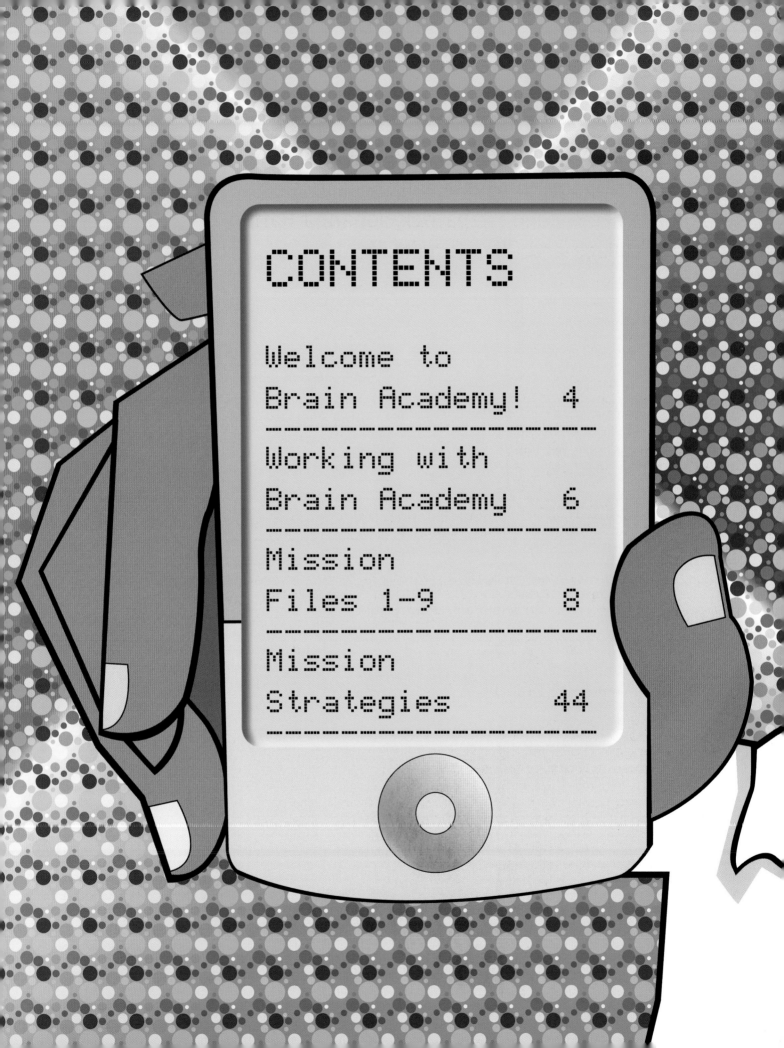

Welcome to Brain Academy!

Welcome to Brain Academy! Make yourself at home. We are here to give you the low-down on the organisation – so pay attention!

It's our job to help Da Vinci and his colleagues to solve the tough problems they face and we would like you to join us as members of the Academy. Are you up to the challenge?

Da Vinci
Da Vinci is the founder and head of the Brain Academy. He is all seeing, all thinking and all knowing – possibly the cleverest person alive. Nobody has ever actually seen him in the flesh as he communicates only via computer. When Da Vinci receives an emergency call for help, the members of Brain Academy jump into action (and that means you!).

Huxley
Huxley is Da Vinci's right-hand man. Not as clever, but still very smart. He is here to guide you through the missions and offer help and advice. The sensible and reliable face of Brain Academy, Huxley is cool under pressure.

Dr Hood
The mad doctor is the arch-enemy of Da Vinci and Brain Academy. He has set up a rival organisation called D.A.F.T. (which stands for Dull And Feeble Thinkers). Dr Hood and his agents will do anything they can to irritate and annoy the good people of this planet. He is a pain we could do without.

Hilary Kumar
Ms Kumar is the Prime Minister of our country. As the national leader she has a hotline through to the Academy but will only call in an extreme emergency. Confident and strong willed, she is a very tough cookie indeed.

General Cods-Wallop
This highly decorated gentleman (with medals, not wallpaper) is in charge of the armed forces. Most of his success has come from the help of Da Vinci and the Academy rather than the use of his somewhat limited military brain.

Mrs Tiggles
Stella Tiggles is the retired head of the Secret Intelligence service. She is a particular favourite of Da Vinci who treats her as his own mother. Mrs Tiggles' faithful companion is her cat, Bond... James Bond.

We were just like you once – ordinary schoolchildren leading ordinary lives. Then one day we all received a call from a strange character named Da Vinci. From that day on, we have led a double life – as secret members of Brain Academy!

Here are a few things you should know about the people you'll meet on your journey.

Inspector Pattern
The trusty Inspector is Buster's right-hand lady. Ms Pattern looks for clues in data and is the complete opposite to the muddled D.A.F.T. agents. Using her mathematical mind to find order where there is chaos, she is a welcome addition to Da Vinci's team. In fact some of the team would do well to think in such a methodical way… a certain Mr Blastov perhaps?

Maryland T. Wordsworth
M.T. Wordsworth is the president of the USA. Not the sharpest tool in the box, Maryland prefers to be known by his middle name, Texas, or 'Tex' for short. He takes great exception to being referred to as 'Mary' (which has happened in the past).

Buster Crimes
Buster is a really smooth dude and is in charge of the Police Force. His laid-back but efficient style has won him many friends, although these don't include Dr Hood or the agents of D.A.F.T. who regularly try to trick the coolest cop in town.

Sandy Buckett
The fearless Sandy Buckett is the head of the fire service. Sandy and her team of brave firefighters are always on hand, whether to extinguish the flames of chaos caused by the demented Dr Hood or just to rescue Mrs Tiggles' cat…

Echo the Eco-Warrior
Echo is the hippest chick around. Her love of nature and desire for justice will see her do anything to help an environmental cause – even if it means she's going to get her clothes dirty.

Victor Blastov

Victor Blastov is the leading scientist at the Space Agency. He once tried to build a rocket by himself but failed to get the lid off the glue. Victor often requires the services of the Academy, even if it's to set the video to record Dr Who.

Prince Barrington
Prince Barrington, or 'Bazza' as he is known to his friends, is the publicity-seeking heir to the throne. Always game for a laugh, the Prince will stop at nothing to raise money for worthy causes. A 'good egg' as his mother might say.

Working with Brain Academy

Do you get the idea? Now you've had the introduction we are going to show you the best way to use this book.

MISSION FILE 1:3

Amazing maps

Time: Hours on end...
Place: In the grounds of Barrington Hall

Prince Barrington has had a magical maze built for visitors to Barrington Hall but he is lost in the maze himself! He needs a map and some map-reading skills to help him out.

I'm having a spot of bother, old chap. Care to lend a hand?

Huxley is on his way. He has a training mission for you.

TM

We can describe squares in the grid using the numbers and letters. So, B3 has a flag in it. Now you do the rest!

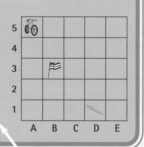

Draw a grid like this.
1) Which square has a pen?
2) Which square has a bike?
3) Draw a sun in C4.
4) Draw a ball in D5.

16

TM

5) Draw a face on your grid in the square below the flag. What is that square called?

6) Draw a sweet 2 squares to the right of the bike. What is this square called?

7) What is above the pen?

8) What is to the left of the ball?

Look at the letter across the bottom of the grid before you look at the number up the side.

Can you use a compass, Bazza? It'll point you in the right direction.

What happened to him?

Of course! I learnt how from my old explorer relative, Sir Shackleton Barrington.

He got lost on the way to the bus stop!

9) Place a counter on the flag.

Move the counter 2 squares south, then 2 squares east, then 4 squares north.

What picture is the counter on now?

Use compass directions to describe at least 2 ways to move:

from A4 to the pen
from E1 to the bike

Don't move over any other pictures.

17

Each mission is divided up into different parts.

The plot
This tells you what the mission is about.

The Training Mission
Huxley will give you some practice before sending you on the main mission.

Each book contains a number of 'missions' for you to take part in. You will work with the characters in Brain Academy to complete these missions.

The Main Mission

This is where you try to complete the challenge.

Huxley's Think Tank

Huxley will give you some useful tips to help you on each mission.

MM

Okay, let's look at your maze, dear Prince.

Start

	1	2	3	4	5	6
F	↓					
E				Dragon's Den		
D						
C					Enchanted Forest	
B					Goblin's Garden	
A	Pixie Party			↓		

Finish

1) Describe how to get from:
   a) the Enchanted Forest to the Goblin's Garden.
   b) the Start to the Dragon's Den.
   c) the Pixie Party to the Finish.

N
W   E
S

MM

2) Plan a route for Prince Barrington.
   He wants to go from the Start to the Pixie Party.

3) Plan a route for Huxley.
   He wants to go from the Start to the Dragon's Den and then to the Enchanted Forest.

4) Plan a route that visits every activity before you leave the maze.

HUXLEY'S THINK TANK
- Remember to use your compass!

Da Vinci files

- Use squared paper to design a maze of your own.
- Put at least 3 activities in your maze.
- Write directions telling visitors how to find each activity and how to find the way out.

No one said this was easy. In fact that is why you have been chosen. Da Vinci will only take the best and he believes that includes you. Good luck!

PS: See pages 44–47 for some hints and tips and a useful process.

The Da Vinci Files

These problems are for the best Brain Academy recruits. Very tough. Are you tough enough?

Station spring clean

Time: Monday morning
Place: The fire station

Every year, Prime Minister Hilary Kumar gives the Golden Hose prize to the team with the cleanest fire station. She is coming to inspect the Brain Academy station this morning but Sandy and her team have been working overtime to clear up the mess from Dr Hood's latest stink bomb campaign. The station is chaotic and Sandy is stressed out!

Last year, D.A.F.T. agents filled all the hoses with mud! I wonder if Buster could lend a hand, this time.

Well, you know what they say, Sandy... a new broom sweeps clean but the old brush knows all the corners!

TM

If we're going to win the Golden Hose, I'll need your help to tidy the station!

1) A red water bucket and a blue water bucket are kept on a shelf.

Write down all the ways they could be arranged.

8

2) A packet of tea bags and coffee are kept in the cupboard.

Write down all the ways they could be arranged.

3) Buster Crimes and Inspector Pattern line up for inspection by Hilary Kumar.

Write down all the ways they could line up.

HUXLEY'S THINK TANK

- What do you notice about the number of answers to parts 1, 2 and 3?
- Make up your own problems with 2 things to put in order to check your answer.
- Can you find any with a different number of orders?
- What if the 2 things are exactly the same?

1) A hammer, an axe and a saw are kept on a shelf.

   Write down all the ways they could be arranged.

2) A whistle, a helmet and a belt are laid out in the fire engine.

   Write down all the ways they could be arranged.

3) A notebook, a pen and a telephone are lined up on the desk.

   Write down all the ways they could be arranged.

HUXLEY'S THINK TANK

- Make up your own problems with 3 things to put in order to check your answer.
- Can you find any with a different number of orders?
- What if 2 of the things are exactly the same, or 3 are the same?

> Sandy and her team are in top shape. 'Golden Hose' winners – congratulations!

Da Vinci files

Investigate putting 4 things in order.

- Start with 4 things that are exactly the same. How many ways can you find?

- Next, try 3 things the same and 1 that is different. How many ways can you find?

- Now, try 2 things the same and 2 that are different. How many ways can you find?

- Finally, try 4 things that are all different. How many ways can you find?

Look for patterns in your results.

Dodgy dominoes

Time: Sunday afternoon
Place: The Brain Academy domino championships

Everyone wants to win the BA Domino Cup. There are games with different sorts of dominoes. Someone wants to win so much that they are cheating... Da Vinci calls in Buster Crimes to help find the culprit!

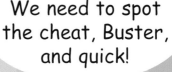
We need to spot the cheat, Buster, and quick!

Cool it, sir! I'm on the case.

If you look at a set of dominoes, you'll see each domino has 2 groups of spots. This domino has a group of 3 spots and 4 spots. In total, the spots add up to 7. Now help me judge the Domino Cup!

1) In Round one, players choose 1 domino each. The person with the highest score wins.

Mrs Tiggles says her total is 12. Huxley says his total is 8 and Bazza says his total is 14.

Who is cheating and who really wins?

Explain how you know.

2) In Round two, players have to work out how many dominoes have a total of 6.

Mrs Tiggles finds 3, Huxley finds 6 and Bazza finds 7.

Who is the winner and who is cheating?

Start by listing the dominoes with a total of 6. The picture above might help you.

3) In Round three, players find the difference between the 2 groups of spots on each domino.

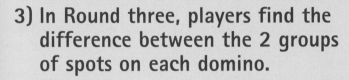

This domino has a difference of 2.
4 – 2 = 2

How many dominoes have a difference of 1?
Mrs Tiggles says 3, Huxley says 4 and Bazza says 6.

Complete the list of dominoes that have a difference of 1.

Who is the winner and who is cheating?

Three!

Four!

Six!

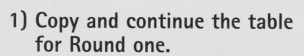

I need some 'cheatfinder' tables!
Can you help?

1) Copy and continue the table for Round one.

Domino total	Ways to make the total	Number of possible ways
0	0 – 0	1
1	0 – 1	1
2	0 – 2 1 – 1	2
3		

HUXLEY'S THINK TANK

- Work from the lowest possible total up to the highest total. Be careful not to miss any out. There are 28 dominoes in the set.

2) Copy and continue the table for Round two.

Domino difference	Ways to make the difference	Number of possible ways
0	0 – 0 1 – 1 2 – 2	

3) For the finals, special sets of dominoes are used.

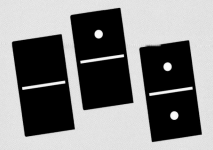

1-spot dominoes

a) A 1-spot set of dominoes can't have more than 1 spot in each group.

Make a cheatfinder table for the differences in a 1-spot set.

b) A 2-spot set of dominoes can't have more than 2 spots in each group.

Make a cheatfinder table for the differences in a 2-spot set.

c) Make cheatfinder tables for the differences in 3-spot, 4-spot and 5-spot sets of dominoes.

2-spot dominoes

What is the pattern for the number of differences? What would the result be for a 9-spot set?

Da Vinci files

- Investigate totals for 1-spot, 2-spot, 3-spot, 4-spot and 5-spot dominoes.
- Try some different spot sets.
- Can you find any quick ways?
- Write down the number of ways to make the totals for a 10-spot set.

Amazing maps

Time: Hours on end...
Place: In the grounds of Barrington Hall

Prince Barrington has had a magical maze built for visitors to Barrington Hall but he is lost in the maze himself! He needs a map and some map-reading skills to help him out.

Huxley is on his way. He has a training mission for you.

I'm having a spot of bother, old chap. Care to lend a hand?

We can describe squares in the grid using the numbers and letters. So, B3 has a flag in it. Now you do the rest!

Draw a grid like this.

1) Which square has a pen?

2) Which square has a bike?

3) Draw a sun in C4.

4) Draw a ball in D5.

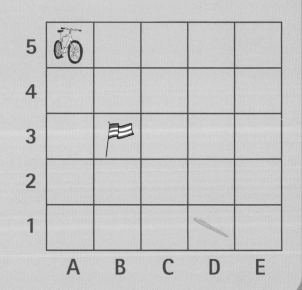

5) Draw a face on your grid in the square below the flag. What is that square called?

6) Draw a sweet 2 squares to the right of the bike. What is this square called?

7) What is above the pen?

8) What is to the left of the ball?

> Look at the letter across the bottom of the grid before you look at the number up the side.

> Can you use a compass, Bazza? It'll point you in the right direction.

> Of course! I learnt how from my old explorer relative, Sir Shackleton Barrington.

> What happened to him?

> He got lost on the way to the bus stop!

9) Place a counter on the flag.

Move the counter 2 squares south, then 2 squares east, then 4 squares north.

What picture is the counter on now?

Use compass directions to describe at least 2 ways to move:

from A4 to the pen
from E1 to the bike

Don't move over any other pictures.

Okay, let's look at your maze, dear Prince.

Start

	1	2	3	4	5	6
F	↓					
E				Dragon's Den		
D						
C					Enchanted Forest	
B					Goblin's Garden	
A	Pixie Party			↓		

Finish

1) Describe how to get from:

   a) the Enchanted Forest to the Goblin's Garden.

   b) the Start to the Dragon's Den.

   c) the Pixie Party to the Finish.

2) Plan a route for Prince Barrington.

   He wants to go from the Start to the Pixie Party.

3) Plan a route for Huxley.

   He wants to go from the Start to the Dragon's Den and then to the Enchanted Forest.

4) Plan a route that visits every activity before you leave the maze.

HUXLEY'S THINK TANK

- Remember to use your compass!

Da Vinci files

- Use squared paper to design a maze of your own.

- Put at least 3 activities in your maze.

- Write directions telling visitors how to find each activity and how to find the way out.

Inspector Pattern's masterclass

Time: 9.00 a.m. sharp
Place: A secret training room at Brain Academy

Inspector Pattern is giving the Brain Academy team some special training. She is showing them how finding patterns in Maths is so useful when solving problems.

The only patterns Maryland can find are on his socks!

You can talk. I've smelt your socks, Huxley, and they're not pleasant!

Right team, let's warm up with these simple sums!

1) How many different sums can you make with these cards?

You don't have to use every card every time.

You can't use a card more than once in each sum.

| + | 3 | 8 | = | – | 5 |

2) How many different sums can you make with these cards?

You don't have to use every card every time.

You can't use a card more than once in each sum.

| 7 | 15 | + | 8 | – | = |

3) Make up some sets of cards that will make the same number of sums as the sets above.

Now there are fewer cards.

1) Find all the sums that make this number sentence true.

How many can you make?

 +   = 3

Okay, now I want you to do these step by step.

2) Find all the sums that make this number sentence true.

How many can you make?

 +   = 4

3) Make all the sums you can with the answer 5...

...then the answer 6
...then the answer 7 and so on!

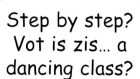

Step by step? Vot is zis... a dancing class?

4) Copy this table and use your findings to finish it.

Answer	1	2	3	4	5	6	7	8
Number of sums you can make	2							

Describe the patterns you can see.

How many sums could you make if the answer was 11?

Check your answer by trying to make all the sums.

HUXLEY'S THINK TANK

- Try to keep the numbers in the sums going up in order so you don't miss any out.

Excellent. Just complete the Da Vinci files to earn yourself a first-class degree!

Da Vinci files

- Try a similar investigation using these cards.
  Your answers should be 0 or above.

  a) 1 – ☐ = ☐

  b) 2 – ☐ = ☐

  c) 3 – ☐ = ☐

- Copy this table and use your findings to finish it.

  Describe the patterns you see.

Starting number	1	2	3	4	5	6	7	8
Number of sums you can make								

- How many sums would you be able to make if the starting number was 11?

  Check your answer by trying to make all the sums.

Happy birthday, James!

Time: Saturday afternoon
Place: Mrs Tiggles' cottage

Mrs Tiggles is having a party for her cat, James Bond.
All his feline friends are invited.

Huxley will help to make the party the cat's whiskers!

I want to give all the guests as much choice as I can.

Only the best for our pussy pals.

These pampered pussies are having their tea. I'm sure they'd prefer 'mice cream' cones!

1) a) Mrs Tiggles has chocolate or mint ice cream. Each guest has 2 scoops.

How many different choices are there?

Write 'C' for chocolate and 'M' for mint, so that you don't need to write the whole word every time.

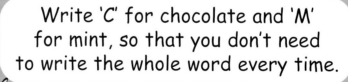

b) Mrs Tiggles has egg or jam sandwiches.
Each guest has 2 sandwiches.

How many different choices are there?

c) The cats have tuna or lamb biscuits. Each cat has
2 scoops of biscuits.

How many different choices are there?

d) What do you notice about the number of choices
when there are 2 to pick from?

2) a) Mrs Tiggles lets each guest choose 2 buns.
She makes cherry buns, iced buns and currant buns.

How many ways are there to pick 2 buns?

b) The cats are allowed 2 toys to take home. There are balls,
string and toy mice.

How many ways are there to pick 2 toys?

HUXLEY'S THINK TANK

- Only change 1 choice at a time
  to help you find them all.

MM

1) Make up your own problem with 3 choices where 2 things are picked each time.

List all the possible choices.

Compare this to when 2 things are picked from 2 choices.

Is it true James drank five bowls of milk?

Yes, he set a new 'lap' record!

2) Mrs Tiggles lets all the cats play in the hall, the garden, the shed and the lounge.

She wants to find James Bond and Fluffy.

List all the places these 2 cats might be.

Start like this:

	Bond	Fluffy
1	Hall	Hall
2	Hall	Garden
3	Hall	

How many answers can you find?

3) Make up your own problem with 4 choices where 2 things are picked each time.

List all the possible options.

What do you notice when 2 things are picked from 4 choices?

Compare this to when 2 things are picked from 2 choices and from 3 choices.

Da Vinci files

Mrs Tiggles has take-home treats in different-coloured bags. Each guest can pick 2 bags.

- Investigate the number of ways guests can pick 2 bags.

Copy and fill in the table to show your results.

Number of different colours	2	3	4	5	6
Number of ways to pick 2 bags	3				

- Explain any patterns you find.

- How many choices would there be with 7 different colours?

Digital dilemma

Time: During a beautiful sunset
Place: Echo's tree house

Da Vinci likes to keep his team on their mental toes. He's asked Echo to make as many numbers as she can with some cards he's found in the storeroom. Echo thinks she may need help if she's going to finish it in time to watch the sunset!

I've got an odd problem that I don't think even you can answer, Huxley.

I'll help you see the light, Echo. Start on the training mission right away!

Our training with Inspector Pattern will help with this. We need to work 'step by step'...

1) Echo has 4 different cards.

| 6 | 3 | 8 | 5 |

a) What is the biggest number she can make with 2 of these cards?

Tens	Units

b) What is the smallest number she can make with 2 of the cards?

c) Use the cards to make as many numbers as you can between the biggest and smallest numbers.

d) Put the numbers in order from the smallest to the biggest.

Remember to think about which digit is in the ten's column!

2) Echo uses the same 4 cards again.

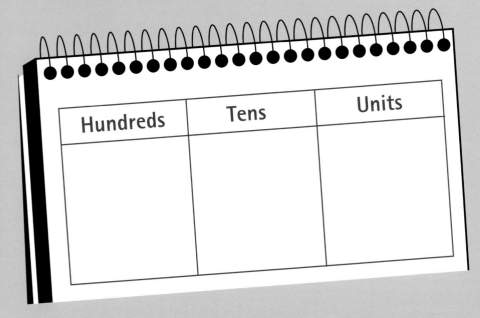

Hundreds	Tens	Units

a) What is the biggest number she can make with 3 cards?

b) What is the smallest number she can make with 3 cards?

c) Use the cards to make at least 6 numbers between the biggest and smallest 3-digit numbers.

d) Put the 3-digit numbers in order from the smallest to the largest.

1) Make these 3 number cards.

| 6 | 1 | 5 |

Copy and complete the table to show all the numbers you can make with these 3 cards.

Hundreds	Tens	Units
		1
	1	5
	1	6
1	5	6

HUXLEY'S THINK TANK

- Make all the numbers starting with a 1 first, then a 5, then a 6.

Sort the numbers you have made into sets like these.

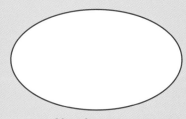

Numbers 1–10

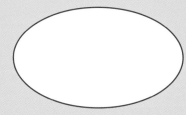

Numbers 11–100

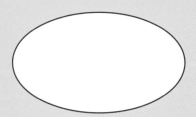

Numbers greater than 100

2) Do the same thing with these 3 number cards.

| 3 | 2 | 8 |

3) Now try with your own sets of 3 number cards. What happens if 2 of your cards are the same?

4) There are 3 piles of cards:
a pile for the number 7
a pile for the number 5
a pile for the number 6

You can use as many of each card as you like.

a) Make all the even 2-digit numbers you can using these cards.

Fill in a table like the one here.

b) Make all the odd 2-digit numbers you can using these cards. Fill in a table.

c) Did you make more odd numbers or more even numbers? Explain why.

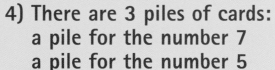

Find the pattern for the number in each set.

Tens	Units

I'm numbered out. I need to sleep and wake up to catch the sunrise.

Da Vinci files

- Choose 3 digits that will make more even numbers than odd numbers.

  Make all the numbers you can, putting them into groups of odd and even numbers.

  Were you right? Explain why.

- Now see what happens with 4 digits.

Pie from the sky!

Time: End of term
Place: General Cods-Wallop's parade ground

General Cods-Wallop is parading his newly trained and smartened up soldiers. Dr Hood wants to spoil it all by dropping blackberry pies from his hot air balloon! General Cods-Wallop has kept the timetable secret to foil the hooded menace.

Fear not, General. The Doctor's plans will crumble if he doesn't know when to drop his deadly desserts.

I don't want those uniforms ruined by a single pie from that fruity fiend!

 1) What time do these clocks show?

a) 4:00

b) 5.15

c)

d)

It's time for you to act. There's not a second to lose!

e) 09.45

f)

g)

2) In the first secret code, all the clocks are 1 hour slow. Write the correct times for each clock now.

3) In the second code, all the clocks are half an hour fast. Write the correct times for each clock now.

4) Write the times shown on these clocks as digital times.

a)

b)

c)

d)

e)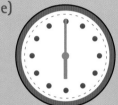

f)

g)

We could have a code like this one that uses the digits in the times. We could add the digits to tell us the hour. 3:15 → 3 + 1 + 5 = 9, so it's 9 o'clock!

03:15

1) Start at 1:00 and keep adding 5 minutes.

How many times can you find that would be 10 o'clock in the General's code?

For example,

1:45 would be 1 + 4 + 5 = 10

1:45 is 10 o'clock in the General's code.

HUXLEY'S THINK TANK

- Keep the times in order, otherwise you might miss some answers.

MM

2) Start at 1:00 and keep adding 1 minute.

How many times can you find that would be 10 o'clock in the General's code?

3) Now try this code where we show two clocks.

The sum of the digits on the first clock tell us the hour. The sum of the digits on the second clock tell us the minutes past the hour.

The first clock shows us that the hour is 1 + 1 + 0 = 2 hours.

The second clock show us that the minutes past is 8 + 2 + 5 = 15 minutes.

That means the time is 2:15.

Try making different times using General Cods–Wallop's idea. How well does it work?

Explain any problems you find.

That was a good idea General, but I think we should make it even more difficult for the pie-hard pest.

4) Let's use the 2 clocks and then put some coins next to them. The coins tell us how many minutes to add to the code time.

So, the first clock shows that the hour is 3 + 2 + 0 = 5 hours.

The second clock shows that the minutes past is 1 + 4 + 5 = 10 minutes.

That means it is 5:10 but the 20p means it is 20 minutes later.

The coded time is 5:30.

Test Da Vinci's idea. How well does this work?

Explain any problems you have.

Hurrumph! That crusty Hood has been foiled again. He'll have to 'pie' harder next time!

Da Vinci files

- Make a timetable for the General's new soldiers. Choose one of the codes to use so that Dr Hood cannot spoil the day and drop pies on the parade.

Happy birthday, Mr President!

Time: Getting late
Place: The Whitehouse

It's the President's birthday party but Maryland T Wordsworth has too much work to do. His desk is hidden under a mountain of paper.

Gee, I'm sorry, I can't come to my own party. I have to sort these papers before Monday.

We'll help you sort out your presidential pickle and get you to the ball!

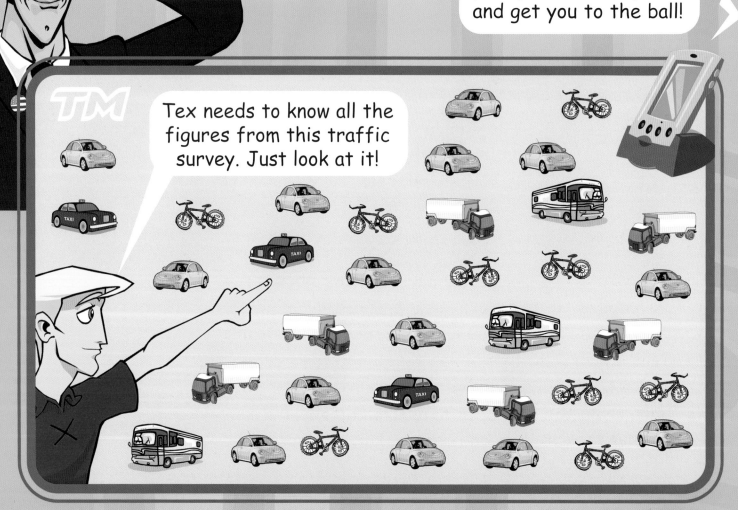

Tex needs to know all the figures from this traffic survey. Just look at it!

1) Information is best if it is sorted into tables and diagrams.

   Draw and complete a tally chart like this to show the President the traffic information.

Vehicle	Tally
car	
lorry	
taxi	III
bus	
bike	

HUXLEY'S THINK TANK

- Remember, for a tally draw 4 lines down, then 1 across them for the number 5. ⦀⦀

2) Now use your tally chart to answer these questions.

   a) Which vehicle was there most of?

   b) How many more bikes were there than buses?

   c) How many taxis and lorries were there altogether?

3) Copy this diagram onto paper.

   Now read this report for Tex and sort the information into the diagram.

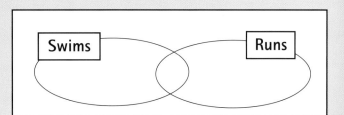

Keeping fit

John runs to school every day and Peter goes swimming twice a week. Jade prefers swimming but sometimes runs with John. Jamal doesn't like water but he wins all the running races. Sue can't get John to go swimming but Ann sometimes goes with her. Peter and Ann both hate running. Sue and Jane prefer to read than go running. Jane can't swim.

Cross out the information as you put it in the diagram.

Now we have to sort out some reports for Tex.

1) Tex got 10 reports today. They were from Buster Crimes, Sandy Buckett and Inspector Pattern.

Buster Crimes sent him the most reports. SandyBuckett sent in the same number of reports as Inspector Pattern.

Use tallies to work out the number or reports they each sent.

Find as many answers as you can.

2) Copy this diagram onto paper.

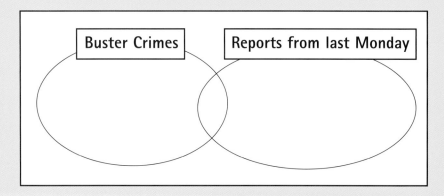

Buster Crimes sent in 3 reports last week.
Tex got 6 reports last Monday.

Fill in the diagram to show this information.

How many different ways can you do this?

3) Tex has an information diagram about secret agents.
This diagram is wrong.

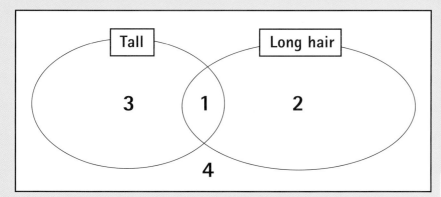

If there are 10 agents, but 4 are not tall
and 3 have long hair, can you fill in the
diagram correctly?

How many ways can you find to fill it in?

I think I'm done,
thanks guys. Now to
get my little ol' party
dress... I mean suit...
from the cleaners!

Da Vinci files

- Make your own information diagram to sort information
  about your friends.

- Decide what information you want to show.

- You might use age, hair colour or eye colour. You might use
  favourite games or lessons.

Nobbled by the Nibblers!

Time: Star date 63406
Place: Victor's workshop

Nibblers from the planet Nobble like to eat numbers. They like numbers that are written on wood best. Victor Blastov needs to make some new Brain Booster bars but can't find a ruler to use. The Nibblers have nibbled the lot!

> Well, Da Vinci. Zere vill be no bars today. I must buy new rulers first.

> I don't think so, Victor. I'll send Huxley to see you right away.

> Stick around, Victor. I know how we can measure this up.

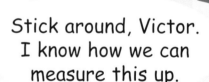

> Let's try estimating first.

1) The Nibblers have left one number on this ruler.

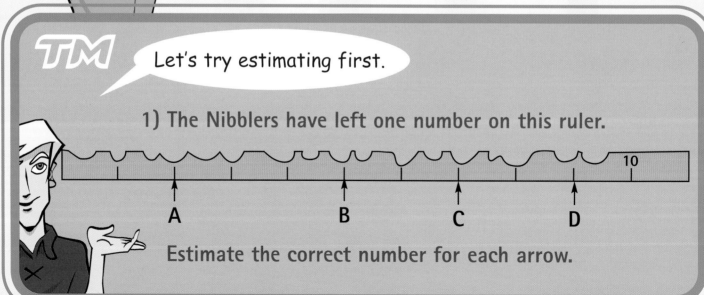

A   B   C   D   10

Estimate the correct number for each arrow.

TM

2) They nibbled the 10s off this metre stick as well.

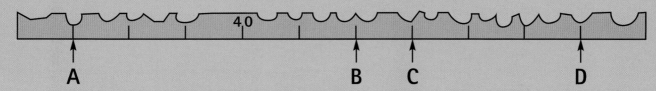

Estimate the correct number for each arrow.

HUXLEY'S THINK TANK

- A good estimate is very close to the correct answer. You need to work it out carefully!

MM

I have a plan. Let's mix up ze numbers as we put zem back on ze metre sticks. Zat vill fool zoze naughty nibblers!

1) Work out the pattern Victor used on these metre sticks.

a)

| 20 | 10 | 40 | 30 | 60 | 50 | 80 | 70 | 100 | 90 |

b)

| 50 | 40 | 30 | 20 | 10 | 100 | 90 | 80 | 70 | 60 |

c)

| 10 | 30 | 50 | 70 | 90 | 20 | 40 | 60 | 80 | 100 |

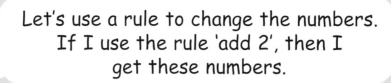

Let's use a rule to change the numbers. If I use the rule 'add 2', then I get these numbers.

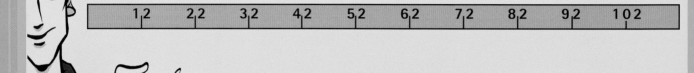

1,2 2,2 3,2 4,2 5,2 6,2 7,2 8,2 9,2 10 2

2) What rule has been used to change the numbers on these metre sticks?

a)

1,5 2,5 3,5 4,5 5,5 6,5 7,5 8,5 9,5 10 5

b)

3,0 4,0 5,0 6,0 7,0 8,0 9,0 100 110 120

c)

6, 1,6 2,6 3,6 4,6 5,6 6,6 7,6 8,6 9,6

d)

2,2 3,2 4,2 5,2 6,2 7,2 8,2 9 2 10 2 11 2

3) Now for a challenge – these have 2-part rules!

a)

1,1 2,3 3,1 4,3 5,1 6,3 7,1 83 91 103

b)

8, 2,2 2,8 4,2 4,8 6,2 6,8 7,2 7,8 8,2 8,8 9,2 9,8

4) Make up 3 rules of your own. Give the number patterns they make to a friend and see if they can work out your rules.

Now I can build ze Brain Booster bars. And by gosh, I zink I need zem after all zis nibbling nuisance!

- Victor has invented some Nibbler-proof tape to stick over numbers. He needs to cut the tape to the correct lengths but has no rulers!

He has pieces of wood 5 cm long and pieces of wood 7 cm long.

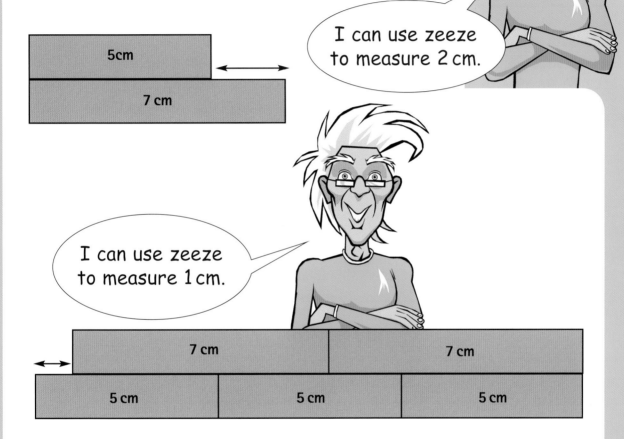

I can use zeeze to measure 2 cm.

I can use zeeze to measure 1 cm.

- How could Victor use the 5 cm and 7 cm pieces of wood to measure every length from 1 cm to 10 cm?

- If Victor had pieces of wood 3 cm, 5 cm and 9 cm long, show how he could measure every length from 1 cm to 20 cm.

Mission Strategies

MISSION FILE 1:1

It may help to use objects, or make pictures of the objects, and try rearranging them. Carefully, write down every different answer you can find. Always check that you don't miss or repeat an answer. Remember that the objects have to be arranged in a straight line, like the class lining up one behind the other!

MISSION FILE 1:2

Make sure you draw the tables so that your findings are easy to read. It is usually better to use squared paper or lined paper when you draw tables because the squares and lines keep the rows and columns evenly spaced. You could make each of the domino sets so that you can check you have found all the possible answers.

MISSION FILE 1:3

When you use grids, always write which column you need before you write the row. In other words, go across before you go up or walk into the house before you climb up the stairs! It is a good idea to draw the compass directions in a corner of your paper to help you solve this Mission. Write your instructions in a list down your page so they are easy to follow. It might help to number them.

MISSION FILE 1:4

You could make cards for this Mission so that you don't use a number or symbol more than once by mistake. Write all your sums in a list down your paper so that your work is easy to check. Try to work through the possible sums in an order so that it is easier to find all the answers. You should be able to find a pattern in your results.

MISSION FILE 1:5

When you are looking for different answers, only change one thing in your list each time. You may find it easier to start with objects so that you can check all the possible choices. Patterns are the key to this Mission. If you can't spot the patterns, check your answers very carefully – you have probably made a mistake somewhere. It is easier to check if you write down every possible choice.

MISSION FILE 1:6

Make a list of odd and even numbers before you start so that you can do quick checks when you need to. Make the columns large enough to write in the digits clearly. When you are thinking about your answers, remember that hundreds are worth more than tens and that tens are worth more than units!

MISSION FILE 1:7

You need to understand digital and analogue times before you start this Mission. It might be a good idea to have a practice clock to use when you are working out the times. When you are finding code times, look for the numbers between 0 and 9 that will make the sum you need (even if you need more than 2 digits) and then try to arrange the digits to make the time.

MISSION FILE 1:8

Check that you know how to tally before starting the Mission. When you draw the Venn diagrams, make sure the overlapping part of the circles is big enough to write in clearly. Remember that the area outside the circles is for answers that don't belong in any of the sets.

MISSION FILE 1:9

Look at a metre stick and think about the spacing between the numbers to help with estimating in this Mission. When you need to explain how the numbers have been arranged, work out what to do to put the numbers back into the proper order and then do the opposite to get the pattern back. Keep puzzling in the Da Vinci files – you can find all the answers!

The TASC Problem Solving Wheel

TASC: Thinking Actively in a Social Context

Learn from experience

Reflect
What have I learned?

What have I learned?

Communicate

Communicate
Who can I tell?

Let's tell someone.

Evaluate

Evaluate
Did I succeed? Can I think of another way?

How well did I do?

Let's do it!

Implement
Now let me do it!

Implement

TA

We can learn to be expert thinkers!

Gather/organise

What do I know about this?

Identify

What is the task?

T A S C

How many ideas can I think of?

Generate

Which is the best idea?

Decide

Gather and Organise
What do I already know about this?

Identify
What am I trying to do?

Generate
How many ways can I do this?

Decide
Which is the best way?

TASC: Thinking Actively in a Social Context © Belle Wallace 2004

nace

What is NACE?

NACE is a charity which was set up in 1984. It is an organisation that supports the teaching of 'more-able' pupils and helps all children find out what they are good at and to do their best.

What does NACE do?

NACE helps teachers by giving them advice, books, materials and training. Many teachers, headteachers, parents and governors join NACE. Members of NACE can use a special website which gives them useful advice, ideas and materials to help children to learn.

NACE helps thousands of schools and teachers every year. It also helps teachers and children in other countries, such as America and China.

How will this book help me?

Brain Academy Supermaths books challenge and help you to become better at learning and a better mathematician by:
- Thinking of and testing different solutions to problems
- Making connections to what you already know
- Making mistakes and learning from them
- Working with your teacher, by yourself and with others
- Expecting you to get better and to go on to the next book
- Learning skills which you can use in other subjects and out of school

We hope that you enjoy the books!

Write to **RISING STARS** and let us know how the books helped you to learn and what you would like to see in the next books.

Rising Stars UK Ltd, 22 Grafton Street, London W1S 4EX